Moneybag And Other Monologues For Lent And Easter

Diana M. Morris

CSS Publishing Company, Inc., Lima, Ohio

For more information about CSS Publishing Company resources, visit our website at www.csspub.com or email us at custserv@csspub.com or call (800) 241-4056.

Cover design by Barbara Spencer
ISBN-13: 978-0-7880-2519-8
ISBN-10: 0-7880-2519-8

PRINTED IN USA

*These skits are dedicated
to all the invisible people
in our lives:
those on the edge of great happenings,
those who do the work, but are never really noticed.
They truly live in the light
of God's unwavering love.*

*They are also dedicated
to my wonderful big sister
Lolita A. Denton*

Table Of Contents

Introduction

This book of biblical skits really started a few years ago when my pastor, Reverend Kerry Reed, asked me to help him write some skits about women of the Bible, which would be used for Lent and Easter. We did do that, but there were so many that we ended up only using women from the New Testament. He wrote half and I wrote the other half. There were eleven or twelve different women and these were used for the Sundays and Wednesdays of Lent. They went over very well. Pat Reed, Kerry's multi-talented wife, did the simple costumes for these people.

In January of 2007, he called again (you do have to watch out when Kerry calls you!) and he asked if I would create skits of the marginalized and invisible people in Jesus' life, death, and resurrection. We met and decided which characters these would be. The choir was going to perform several of the Sundays. That eliminated the skits on those Sundays, which is why there are only nine skits.

I tried to live with these people in my mind after searching the scriptures (NIV) and reading different translations. I researched the culture of that time. It was fun to give names to these Greek and Roman characters, as well as those from Jerusalem. They were all researched.

I did combine the centurion from two different times: the centurion with no name who asks Jesus to heal his servant and the centurion at the cross. I also put these skits in various letter-writing forms. The centurion writes to his sister and Rome and she reads it aloud. In this way, he is seated and speaking as he writes from Jerusalem and she enters, reading the letter aloud, in Rome.

There are very few props: a moneybag, a flower stand or table, and some gold coins (foil-covered chocolate ones could be used) for one skit and a quill pen, pieces of paper, a small table and a chair for the centurion skit. We didn't have the actors memorize their lives; they were allowed to use their scripts.

I hope that you will use these as a starting point for youth groups or Sunday services, especially for Lent and Easter. After I finished them, I noticed that all were appropriate for the Easter season. In any case, enjoy these skits and think of all those invisible people within our lives.

— Reverend Diana M. Morris

Two Blind Men

Lent 1
A Dialogue

Two Blind Men
Deuteronomy 26:1-11

Characters
Aaron — middle-aged man
Jacob — middle-aged man

Props
None required

Setting
None required

Costumes
Use period costumes — robes, sandals, head coverings, and the like

(Jacob comes in from the aisle and Aaron comes from the side aisle to meet at the chancel area. They have not seen each other for a long time. They embrace.)

Aaron: *(ironically)* My old friend, it's so good to *see* you.

Jacob: *(chuckles, then says ironically)* And for me to *see* you, Aaron. What is it now, five years?

Aaron: Yes, and four of those since Jesus' resurrection. It doesn't seem possible. How are you?

Jacob: I'm better now than I was. After I regained my sight, I couldn't figure out what I could do for a living. What was I to do? How *was* I to live and where? After all, I was born blind and never learned a trade. I only learned how to beg at the gate.

Aaron: I understand. At least I had learned carpentry before I lost my sight. But what did you do?

Jacob: A new friend, one who was following Jesus, helped me learn to be a shepherd. Shepherds are treated as badly as those of us who have to beg for a living. But, being a shepherd taught me more about Jesus' teachings and more about his parables. After a while I started following some of Jesus' disciples instead of tending sheep. I still find it amazing that our Lord rose from the dead! But I know it's true.

Aaron: I've been with Paul and a few others when they went to Corinth and then back to Jerusalem. I must ask you, though, are you still amazed at so much beauty to see? The beauty of the stars at night, water droplets that magnify rainbows, flowers and cypress trees, sunrises and sunsets — all of it is overwhelming at times.

Jacob: What amazes me all the time is the beauty in peoples' faces, each of them with such different personalities, and all the different animals. Then there is the sweetness of small children, especially when they are sleeping — or even if the child is wide awake and crying!

Aaron: That's all true. I still remember the very first thing I saw. I saw the face of Jesus. Do you remember that?

Jacob: I could never forget. His face just reflected love and compassion. Yet, the decision of our healing was up to us, he said, and our faith and belief that Jesus was the Son of God. How could we have known when we called out to him to heal us that it wasn't just our sight he would heal?

Aaron: I've often wondered what would have happened if we had listened to the crowd yelling at us to be quiet? If we had not called out, where would we be now? We had heard of Jesus and that he was coming our way.

Jacob: Yes, and when we heard about him, we believed right away that he was the chosen one, the Messiah.

Aaron: But we couldn't keep quiet and even the crowd saw our healing. We had to go and tell everyone that the Messiah healed us — that we could see!

Jacob: I wish some of the things we didn't have to see, like those who didn't have the chance to see Jesus as we did and those who are empty inside, who have no life within them. But the worst sight was seeing Jesus crucified. Do you remember how dark it became as he died? For a moment I thought I was losing my sight again because it was only three o'clock in the afternoon.

Aaron: I, too, thought I was losing my sight again as I stood there and watched him take his last breath. But later, the next week, I heard that Jesus had risen from the grave and once again, immediately actually, I believed it. He was, and is, my Lord. I'll travel with his other followers to tell everyone all he taught us and who he is.

Jacob: I must go. I'm meeting with some of his followers yet this afternoon and as you know, we have to be careful where we meet and who we tell about him. But I, too, can hardly contain myself about my Lord and Savior, Jesus Christ. Shalom, my friend, and may we meet again soon.

Aaron: Shalom, Jacob. God go with you!

(They leave the opposite way from where they came in.)

Moneybag

Lent 2
A Monologue

Simon,
Brother Of Jesus

Lent 2
A Midweek Monologue

Moneybag
Luke 13:31-35

Character

Moneybag (offstage voice)

Props

Table
Moneybag
Coins
Microphone

Setting

Stage with spotlight

Costume

None required

(A moneybag is sitting on a table in the center of the chancel area with coins on it, around it, and down on the floor. A spotlight is on the moneybag and the person doing the monologue is out of sight with a microphone.)

Moneybag: You might wonder what a moneybag is doing talking to you in this season of Lent, a time when we think about Jesus and his trip to Jerusalem. Well, Jesus and money were always intertwined, from his birth and the rich gifts he was given, to his betrayal by Judas. And Judas — taking the thirty silver coins given to him by the Sanhedrin — asked these men to take back the money. But they would not take it back. "I have sinned," he said, and, "I have betrayed innocent blood." It was at this time that Judas threw the coins on the floor and back to the Pharisees.

What do we know about the money of Jesus' day? We know that there were two kinds of coins. The first were the Roman coins marked with an image of Caesar and the second were the temple coins used by the moneychangers in the outer part of the temple. That was where Roman money was exchanged for Jewish coins. There is something about me that was true in Jesus' time and is still true in the present time. There is never enough of me. If you are poor and can hardly pay the bills, you want more money. Likewise, when you have a lot of money, you still want more of it. There is never enough of me. People always want more and more.

Did you know that Jesus actually talked about money more than anything else? The money issue was in his parables, in his teachings, and in his life from the beginning until he took a whip and chased all of those moneylenders out of the temple at Jerusalem.

Jesus saw to it that Judas handled the money for Jesus and his followers, as a group. Isn't it interesting that we never hear of Judas being qualified to handle money? And yet, we hear about Matthew being a former tax collector. Obviously, he was qualified to handle money even when he cheated lots of people as a tax collector.

All of the disciples, not just Judas, complained about the extravagance of the ointment that the woman used to anoint Jesus' feet and head. It wasn't just Judas who complained. These disciples believed that this could have been sold and the proceeds given to the poor. It was worth a year's wages. Judas did not say this because he cared about the poor, but because he was a thief; as keeper of the moneybag, he used to help himself to what was put in.

Jesus, himself, had no money. When he was crucified, he had no money, just his cloak, and the guards rolled dice to see who would win it.

I remember well the parable about the man who issued coins to his three workers, giving the first man ten coins, the second man five coins, and the third man one coin. These men were to invest these coins and make more money for the master. The first two men did make more money for their employer, but the third man was afraid of losing his one coin and therefore, he buried it. The two men who made money were told that they were good and faithful servants. The third man was called a lazy and wicked servant and even his one coin was taken away from him.

I have often wondered what the man who owned the pigs felt about Jesus. You remember that story, the herd of pigs was invaded by evil spirits, so Jesus told the spirits to leave and then the herd of pigs ran off the cliff and was killed. Did Jesus think about the cost of all these pigs and what it would do to their owner? We don't know from the story, but I bet Jesus did know the cost.

One day, Jesus gave the people the blessings you call the Beatitudes. He told the disciples that the people, about 5,000 of them, plus women and children, were hungry and needed fed. He asked the disciples to feed the 5,000, but the disciples did not know how they could do this. Judas told them that they didn't have that much money, and the others agreed. They told Jesus to send the people away. Jesus was then given two little fish and five loaves of bread. He blessed them and then asked the disciples to give that meager amount of food to the crowd. They did, and they had twelve baskets left over. Remember, when you share of me there is always more than enough.

Many cruel things have been done to people because of me — because of money! There have been wars, robberies, greed, and deaths. The crusades were some of the worst of the wars and deaths because of me. Some of the thousands who were killed in just the last century, and even the current wars, are all for money in one way or another. However, most of these things are because of the *love* of money. Money, itself, isn't bad or sinful; money can do so much good.

Do you want to be me or another bag of money in either coins or paper bills? Do you want to be rich and have enough? What would you do to have a moneybag of your own? Think before you answer, for each decision you make about money is a time of crossroads, a time of decision.

Think before you answer!

(Spotlight turns off immediately after the last word is spoken.)

Simon, Brother Of Jesus
Matthew 13:10-17

Character
Simon — young adult male

Props
None required

Setting
None required

Costume
Simon is dressed shepherd-like — sandals, head covering, and so on

Simon: You've heard many things about two of my brothers. There were five brothers in my family and several sisters, and you've probably never even heard their names. The women of my time were considered of no use, even though they kept the house, taught the early lessons to the children, sewed clothes, and so on.

One of my brothers changed the world, not just in my time, but forever, and in every land. My next oldest brother followed in the first one's footsteps, at least as well as he was able. The five brothers were James, Joseph, Judas, Jesus, and me. My name is Simon. Jesus was the firstborn and I was the last of all the brothers and sisters. I'm the baby of the family. I was very young, a teenager you would call me now, when Jesus was baptized. It was at that time that he was gone in the wilderness for a long time. Some of the family thought he was dead. However, when he came back from the wilderness, he was changed.

Almost from the very beginning, the Jewish authorities were upset with my big brother. I couldn't understand this because I had always looked up to Jesus. He was an accomplished carpenter, too. He was so loving and caring about each of us. Our village of Nazareth loved him. However, with our father, Joseph, dead, the villagers couldn't understand why Jesus would go away, why he was not married, and why he didn't stay to help his mother to whom he had always been the closest. It wasn't until after Jesus was crucified and then arose from the grave that James became the leader of the church in Jerusalem. So, you see, the two oldest brothers didn't live as was expected of them. Our family was full of different crossroads. We children heard people talk about mother being with child before she and my father were married.

Then again, it was interesting, too, that as the church grew, so did the stories about Jesus. People would ask our mother, Mary, about Jesus. Was he born at home, was he sick as a baby, and is that why Mary, Joseph, and Jesus went to Egypt for several years? So the stories began and were added to, at times. I always thought there was something special about my big brother, but in a kind way. I heard that the family went to hear Jesus, and then wanted to take him home because they thought he was crazy. Jesus rebuked them all. Our family was outraged that he would treat our mother that way. However, although she was hurt, she understood and they went back to Nazareth. It was later that our mother started following Jesus and listening to her oldest son. She remained faithful as she saw him beaten, crucified, and buried. She even held her dead son in her arms before they took him to a tomb owned by a very rich man, named Joseph of Arimathea, a member of the Sanhedrin. She was also there to see the empty tomb and then to see Jesus in the upper room. No one but the family knows that he came to say good-bye to all of us, too. By that time we knew that yes, he was human, and yes, he was the Son of God.

Crippled Woman

Lent 3
A Monologue

Centurion Darius
And His Sister, Cassia

Lent 3
A Midweek Skit

Crippled Woman
Luke 13:10-17

Character
Rachel — middle-aged woman

Props
None required

Setting
None required

Costume
Rachel is dressed in period clothing

Rachel: Hello, my name is Rachel and my story brings a lot of people to a crossroads in their lives. You see, several things happened over eighteen years. You'll hear me talking about my childhood friend, Adah. You'll hear about several people in my story.

Let's start eighteen years and one month ago. Adah told me that she saw the very beginning of my illness. I was having a hard time standing up straight and to do so was extremely painful, so I would bend over just a little bit to relieve the pain. Over the weeks and months and years, I ended up doubled over. The children made fun of me and I felt hopeless, defeated, like a failure, and very depressed. I had been to many physicians and healers over the years. I had to have help with everything: dressing, cleaning myself, cooking, even eating, and all of the things that we take for granted in our normal day. I did not marry because no one would have me and therefore I had no children because it would have been physically impossible. Most of the people in my village felt that I had a physical demon and that it was contagious, which wasn't true.

My story is intertwined with Jesus of Nazareth, but those who wrote about him did not think that my story was important enough to tell what the name of my village was, or even that I had a name. I've taken a name just so I can tell you my story. I was not contagious, which they found out after weeks and months. Therefore, I was not shunned like those with leprosy were. In your time, there is a name for my disease. It is called Ankylosing Spondylitis (ankle-lo-sing spon-dil-i-tis) and even though 2,000 years have past since Jesus was on earth, there is still no cure for this painful disease. The disease is a form of progressive arthritis with inflammation and stiffness. Eventually, the spinal bones fuse together, which makes my story even more of a miracle! All that can be done for the people with this disease is to try to manage their pain. My spine had fused entirely and I was bent over double, which is very bad for the rest of your body and its organs. Literally, I was bound by my body, virtually bound with invisible chains of calcium that had hardened my spine.

I'm not sure why I went to the synagogue that sabbath day. I did not go often because of the jeering from the children and just because it was so painful to get there. I was in the back of the congregation, in back of all the women, actually, but I couldn't be invisible appearing the way I did. To act like I wasn't there was impossible. I had heard about this Jesus. Reports of his teachings were rampant throughout the village, but I didn't go to the synagogue for him to heal me because I'd given up after so many doctors and healers were unable to do anything for me.

Jesus had just finished one of his teaching stories, the last one according to Luke's writings, then he got up and called my name to come to him. Most people who were healed went searching for Jesus. I did not. Everyone was watching and wondering what I'd done to get this specific attention. I really couldn't see Jesus well because I was bent double. My depression about my illness and my pain was a great deal like a physical demon. There was a hush over all the crowd as I inched my way forward and my friend, Adah, touched my hand as I moved forward, giving me comfort. I will never forget that moment. Jesus said to me, "Woman, you are set free from your infirmity" and then he laid his hands on my back and *immediately*, with no hesitation, I stood up straight. I could take the first good breath that I'd had in years and years. Then I began to praise God! I gave my all in praise of God and of my healing through Jesus. The crowd was grinning from ear to ear, my friends were praising God, and some were laughing. My friend, Adah, was crying and laughing at the same time.

Then the funniest thing happened, at least I thought it was funny. I saw that the leader of the synagogue was angry and the more he acted out his anger, the more I praised God. But Jesus was angry with this man and told him that he was a hypocrite! This leader said it was unlawful to heal on the sabbath according to the Fourth Commandment. Jesus said to him and his followers, "Does not each one of you on the sabbath untie his ox or his donkey from the manger and lead it out for watering? This daughter of Abraham, who has been bound for eighteen years now, ought she not to have been set free on the sabbath day from this bondage?" Indeed, when Jesus had said these things, his adversaries were humiliated and the whole crowd rejoiced at all the splendid deeds done by Jesus.

Then, Adah and I were walking and dancing together, for I was healed! I was healed by the power of God through Jesus. Now you know the rest of my story!

It troubles me, though, because I've heard some rumors that the authorities are trying to snare Jesus. I understand he's going to Jerusalem soon. I pray for Jesus constantly. Maybe you should, too.

Centurion Darius
And His Sister, Cassia
Matthew 8:5-14, 27-54; Mark 15:39

Characters
> Darius
> Cassia

Props
> Table and chair
> Papers and pen

Setting
> None required, but a spotlight could focus on the speaking character as the scene switches back and forth

Costumes
> Use costumes from the period

(Darius is seated at a table, writing a letter, and speaking as he writes.)

Darius: Dear Cassia,

I hope this finds you well. Thank you for your last letter telling me how our parents are. You are such a good listener through these letters. I can tell because you seem to write back to me as soon as you receive a letter.

I have been very troubled of late. I told you several letters ago of how ill my manservant, Faustus, has been. Well, now I must tell you about his healing and tell you the end of the story.

Several weeks ago, one of my soldiers informed me that there was an itinerant Hebrew preacher who was also noted for his ability to heal. They told me his name was Jesus and that his hometown was Nazareth. It's just a very little village and not noted for anything in particular. They said he was very close right now, even though he has been wandering all over Galilee and was slowly heading south toward Jerusalem. I went looking for him and found him just as he was coming into Capernaum. I said to him, "Lord, my servant, Faustus, lies at home paralyzed and in terrible suffering." Jesus told me that he would come with me and heal him, but I told him that was not necessary, that I didn't deserve to have him come under my roof. I told him that I was a man under authority, with soldiers under me and that if I tell one to "go," he goes; or to "come," and he comes to my command. Jesus seemed astonished at my faith and said so to his followers. Then he told me to go back home and I would find my servant well. And when I got home, Faustus was healed! *(fades out as Cassia picks up)*

(Cassia quietly enters from the other side of the stage, reading Darius' letter. She picks up where he has faded out.)

Cassia: I knew that this man was a prophet of the Hebrew people. Once in a while, I heard about his healings, but he never seemed to make any problems for my soldiers and me. That changed one Sunday afternoon. A crowd of people started taking off their cloaks and laying them on the road into Jerusalem. They did this waving palm branches, you know, the big ones. Then I saw Jesus riding in on a donkey. To tell the truth my soldiers said he looked rather ridiculous as his legs were almost on the ground because the donkey was so short. They said the people were hailing him with the phrase, "Hosanna! Blessed is the King of Israel that comes in the name of the Lord." *(fades out as Darius picks up)*

Darius: There were not that many people and it really lasted a short time. It wasn't until the next day that things began to change. Jesus walked into the Jewish temple and started a ruckus with a whip. He began to chase out all the moneychangers and the sellers of animals for sacrifice. Nothing else happened, but because of the uproar, Pilate ordered more troops onto the streets to quell any more problems. All the soldiers were upset with more work, and it was beginning to feel like a tightrope. The Jews began to celebrate their holiday on Thursday night. Only thirty of my cohorts had to be near Pilate. That night, Jesus was arrested in a garden and taken to the Jewish authorities, called the Sanhedrin. They forced him to go to Pilate who could find no fault with him. But these particular authorities wanted Jesus crucified and on Friday morning they had encouraged many of the crowd to ask Pilate to crucify him. *(fades out as Cassia picks up)*

Cassia: I was told to take care of the crucifixion of Jesus and the two other men who were thieves. First, my men tied Jesus to a post and proceeded to whip him. He was so bloody and weak. They also made fun of him by making a crown of thorns and placing it on his head so that these large thorns were forced into his scalp and forehead. They gave him a robe and a palm branch and then they spat on him. When they took the robe off, his wounds started to bleed all over again. Then it was time to take him to that hill that was really the city dump. The people called it Golgotha or "the place of the skull." As we marched the three men up to that hill, they were also made to carry their crosspiece on their shoulders. Jesus stumbled twice and the second time I grabbed this strong-looking fellow to carry Jesus' cross. I noticed that he had two boys with him, but that didn't stop me. *(fades out as Darius picks up)*

Darius: It took several groups of my men to get the three men nailed to their crosses. It seemed that Jesus was hallucinating, be-cause he kept talking to his "father" and there was no male there that would have been his father. As a matter of fact, there was one man about Jesus' age with a group of about three or four women right at the foot of the cross. Someone told me that one of the women was his mother. I don't understand how she could have stood there to watch this cruel and horrible form of dying. I kept listening to his words, and I kept thinking about my servant, Faustus, that Jesus had healed. Why was this good man being put to death? I would have given anything to not be there. However, that was what I was ordered to do and there was no way I could change that. At close to three o'clock in the afternoon, Jesus said, "It is finished," and appeared to have died. I took my sword and put it in his side and blood came out, but there was no movement of his body. *(fades out as Cassia picks up)*

Cassia: Do you remember when I was hurt when we were children and the large scar that I had ever since then? Well, when Jesus' blood sprayed on me, it touched that scar and then healed it! *(acts surprised)* I just couldn't believe it even though I knew that he had healed Faustus from afar. Anyway, I remember saying, "Truly this man was the Son of God." I said it, but I wasn't sure what all that meant until later. But that wasn't the end of it. Two of the Jews from the Sanhedrin had gone to Pilate to ask for the body of Jesus and to bury him in a brand-new tomb belonging to one of them. I think his name was Joseph. *(fades out as Darius picks up)*

Darius: I thought this would be the end of these happenings. But other Jews were worried that Jesus' disciples would carry the body away because Jesus had said that he would rise again. I was called to see Pilate and he asked that I put a guard on the tomb for several days and nights. The first night was uneventful, but on Sunday morning at dawn, my guards felt a mighty earthquake and saw a bright light. The stone was rolled away of its own accord. My men were frightened and they hurried back to inform me and then I had to tell Pilate! It's too long a story to tell you what became of those few soldiers of mine. On the day Jesus died, because it was their sabbath, they did not have time to bury him with the burial spices, so on Sunday, at dawn, a small group of women came to where the tomb was. They went into the tomb, but Jesus wasn't there! I'm told that they hurried back to Jesus' disciples to tell them. Cassia, I must tell you this, but you must not tell a soul, because it could end my life and the lives of many others: I have become a follower of Jesus. I, too, believe that Jesus rose from the dead that morning and is alive, and some day those of us that believe — Jew and Gentile — will be with him in the next life. I want to get back to

Rome to tell you all about this Jesus, this Son of God, the only God. *(fades out as Cassia picks up)*

Cassia: I want to tell you the whole story about Jesus and his teachings and his gift of new life with God. One more thing, the Jewish temple has a place that only the rabbi may go into and it is called the "holy of holies." There is a curtain between this place and the rest of the worship area. When Jesus died, at that very moment in the darkest skies you've ever seen at three o'clock in the afternoon, the curtain in the temple was torn in two. One of Jesus' disciples, named Peter, explained from that moment, no one had to come to God through an intercessor. Because Jesus died for each of us, now we can each come to God — this holy God, who gave his precious Son, on our own. *(fades out as Darius picks up)*

Darius: Be well, Cassia. My love to you, dear sister. If I do not see you in this lifetime, then I will see you in the next one!

Zacchaeus

Lent 4
A Skit

Nicodemus And Joseph Of Arimathea

Lent 4
A Midweek Dialogue

Zacchaeus
Luke 15:1-3, 11b-32; 19:1-10

Characters
    Zacchaeus
    Narrator
    Grandchild 1
    Grandchild 2
    Grandchild 3

Props
    Chair

Setting
    None required

Costumes
    Use costumes of the period

(Zacchaeus, a short man, stands in front of a chair. When Narrator begins to talk, Zacchaeus sits down on a chair.)

Zacchaeus: Hello! You will know me by the children's story that will be told to you. Just remember, there is more to me than being in a tree! Here is my story, told by my grandchildren.

Narrator: *(stands off to the side)* This is the story of Zacchaeus.

(Grandchildren are quietly standing in front of Zacchaeus.)

Grandchild 1: Zacchaeus was a little man who wanted to see Jesus. He wasn't tall. He was very small.

Grandchild 2: One day, Zacchaeus heard that Jesus was coming to Jericho.

Grandchild 3: He heard them say he was coming that day.

Narrator: Zacchaeus decided to go where Jesus would be. He decided to go to Jericho. As Zacchaeus came near the place where Jesus was walking, he saw crowds of people.

Grandchild 3: People were there from everywhere. Zacchaeus tried to push his way through the crowd. He tried to get through. It was too hard to do.

Grandchild 2: Zacchaeus was determined to find another way to see Jesus. He looked around. No way could be found. Finally, Zacchaeus climbed a sycamore tree along the path.

Grandchild 1: He climbed that tree, Lord Jesus to see.

Narrator: When Jesus came to the sycamore tree, he called to Zacchaeus.

Grandchild 3: Climb down from the tree. You are special to me.

Narrator: Jesus told Zacchaeus to hurry because he was going to his house.

Grandchild 2: Come, keep up the pace. Let's hurry to your place.

Narrator: Zacchaeus welcomed Jesus gladly. Follow me. My guest you'll be.

Grandchild 1: Zacchaeus felt nine feet tall that day. He was a little man, but he felt so grand.

Narrator: Zacchaeus told Jesus,

Grandchild 2: Lord, here and now, I give half of my possessions to the poor, and if I have cheated anybody, I will pay them back four times the amount. I'll give half to the poor. To the others, I'll pay more.

Grandchild 1: He has repented.

Grandchild 2: He has been saved.

Grandchild 3: Alleluia! Alleluia!

All Grandchildren: Amen! Amen![1]

Zacchaeus: Well, by now you know that I am Zacchaeus! And I'm known around Jericho and different parts of Palestine to have kept my promises. I gave away my fortune and yes, most of it had been made by cheating. But I often wonder what my life would have been like if I had not encountered Jesus that day.

Would I have cared later when I heard he was crucified? And later still when I heard he was raised from the dead? Would I have believed?

Well, I've talked with his disciples so often since that wonderful day. The twelve are no longer twelve, but hundreds of believers. All of them are hearing about Jesus, his life and his teachings from Jerusalem to Rome. Many of the followers have to meet in secret because the authorities are trying to get rid of them and their gospel teachings. But it can't be stopped! After all, Jesus is the Son of God! And that's what I tell anyone who will listen.

But, let me go back to my questions and my fortune. If I had continued as a tax collector for the Romans, I would have continued to cheat others and would have been such a hard, unforgiving man who would have treated his wife and family cruelly, including my wonderful grandchildren, as strangers. After my encounter with Jesus and his coming to my house, "a sinner's house," I now know my family and cherish each of them and the new friends I've made. I am no longer hated. I am no longer a stranger to those who loved me and who love me still.

Jesus was right when he said, "Today salvation has come to this house, because this man, too, is a son of Abraham. For the Son of Man came to seek and to save what was lost." The Son of God came to me, Zacchaeus, and I am no longer lost.

Thanks be to God!

---

1. Connie Walters, *Reader's Theater Bible-based Dramas New Testament* (Grand Rapids, Michigan: School Specialty Publishing, 1995), pp. 63-64.

Nicodemus And Joseph Of Arimathea
John 3:1-9; 7:19-39; 19:38-39

Characters
> Narrator
> Nicodemus
> Joseph

Props
> None required

Setting
> None required

Costumes
> Use costumes of the period

(Nicodemus and Joseph of Arimathea come to the area around the pulpit. When Narrator begins to speak, the two men freeze. When Narrator is finished, then the men are animated again and walk to the middle of the chancel area.)

Narrator: These two men, Joseph of Arimathea and Nicodemus, are walking through the garden away from the tomb. Sabbath has already begun; Joseph has just had a tomb built for himself in the stone of the garden. They have just finished preparing Jesus' body for death using the expensive ointments that Nicodemus brought.

Nicodemus: Joseph, I'm so grateful that your servants were able to help us with the stone, but I'm also pleased that you dismissed them before Shabbos began. It makes no difference about the two of us, as we are unclean anyhow with having touched Jesus' body. The seal mixture should keep that stone in place for eternity.

Joseph: The stone was far too heavy for the two of us and the soldiers wouldn't help anymore. It was luck that their centurion, I believe his name was Darius, ordered them to help us get Jesus down from the cross. Hopefully, my servants got back home in time for Shabbos. At least they didn't have to touch the body.

Nicodemus: I didn't think it would end this way.

Joseph: Nor did I. Oh, how I wish that I had come forward sooner, but I was too afraid of losing my position, my riches, my seat on the Sanhedrin, and my role as teacher. It's all gone now, but I was not going to let Jesus' body hang there for the birds and weather as the other Roman criminals. He was my Lord and I finally had to take a stand. I lost my fear of being known as a follower. I had to see Pilate and go into his quarters. I guess I became unclean when I did that. I was remembering how Jesus said that you were not unclean by what you took into your mouth but by what comes out of your mouth. This day was a time of crossroads for both of us. Our lives will never be the same.

(Joseph and Nicodemus freeze.)

Narrator: One of the legends of Joseph was that after the resurrection, at the behest of Peter, Joseph was adopted as one of the 72 disciples. After that he departed for Rome, and was encountered with many hazards on the sea. It is also said that he then went on to Britain to bring the gospel to all.

(Joseph and Nicodemus become animated again.)

Nicodemus: I finally came out of the shadows, too. Why didn't I do this earlier? Maybe it would have made a difference in swaying some of the other members of the Sanhedrin. I thought I was courageous when I said to the others not to rush to judgment about Jesus. Maybe Jesus would not have had to die. Where will all of his followers go?

Joseph: I don't know. It was shameful that more of his followers were not at the crucifixion, but I know they were afraid. John was there with Jesus' mother, Mary, and a few of the other women. But where were the men? I was afraid this afternoon when the earthquake happened along with the darkness and the rain. I wonder if the disciples heard and saw the same things?

Nicodemus: The disciples were afraid, as well they should be. The authorities, Jewish and Roman, will be looking for them. Did you notice a very small stream of water mixed with Jesus' blood? It seemed significant somehow.

(Joseph and Nicodemus freeze.)

Narrator: Both men became bold in witnessing for Jesus' resurrection, but at this particular time, just after his burial, they thought everything was finished.

(Joseph and Nicodemus become animated again.)

Joseph: Nicodemus, do you remember when you first heard and saw Jesus? I ask because I am so glad that you told me about him. If you hadn't, I probably would not have gone to hear him. He truly was the Son of God, and yet, how could he be dead if that is true? Is this the way the Messiah dies?

Nicodemus: I wish I had the answer to that question. About a year ago, I heard that he was teaching around Bethany, so basically I just followed the crowd. I stayed back because I just wanted to listen. I was curious. However, I didn't want to intrude with my clothes indicating that I was a member of the Sanhedrin. What if he really was ... well, you know. I'm sure you felt that way, too, Joseph.

Joseph: Yes, I also wondered if he really could be the Messiah. But I didn't dare say so in the council. Is that the only time you saw Jesus?

Nicodemus: The first time I went by night to see and talk with him. I didn't want to be seen, but I had to talk to him. I told him that I believed that he was a great teacher for all the signs and healings he had done, and he began to tell me that I must be born again! I'm still not sure what that means, because physically it's impossible.

(Joseph and Nicodemus freeze.)

Narrator: Legend has it that Nicodemus was baptized by Peter and John. But then for some reason, he was banned from Jerusalem during the Jewish uprising and the stoning of Stephan. An aprocryphal writing is credited to him, which is simply called, "The Gospel of Nicodemus."

(Joseph and Nicodemus become animated again.)

Joseph: Nicodemus, it seems that we have forsaken our religion by wrapping and burying the crucified body of our Lord. What would you suggest we do now?

Nicodemus: Let's find the disciples and ask to hear their stories and the teachings of Jesus. It would be wonderful to just hear them again. Maybe they have an idea of what we all should do now.

Joseph: Look, Nicodemus! That group of soldiers seems to be coming toward the tomb. Surely they won't disturb the seal!

Nicodemus: I wonder why they want to go to a dead man's tomb?

Alexander And Rufus:
Sons Of
Simon Of Cyrene

Lent 5
A Midweek Skit

Alexander And Rufus:
Sons Of Simon Of Cyrene
Matthew 27:32-37

Characters

Mother — wife of Simon of Cyrene, mother of Alexander and Rufus, about sixty years of age

Alexander — about 15 years of age

Rufus — about 10 years of age

Props

Chairs

Setting

Their home in Jerusalem, around 48 AD

Costumes

All are dressed in common clothes from that time period

(Mother is sitting on a chair, reminiscing about past times. Alexander and Rufus are on the opposite side of the stage.)

Rufus: Father, come back! Come back!

Alexander: Rufus, it will be okay.

Rufus: But where are they taking him? Why did they make him carry that man's crosspiece? Are they going to crucify Father, too?

Alexander: Rufus, come with me and just slip back in the crowd. We'll follow them up to where they are crucifying those men. I think Father is supposed to carry that crosspiece. I'm sure they are not going to hurt him.

(Alexander and Rufus freeze as Mother speaks.)

Mother: I can still hear my sons, telling that story over and over again when they returned to Cyrene with Simon. It's been many, many years ago, and Simon has been gone quite a few years. I know he's with our Lord. Listen again with me, to the story they tell.

(Mother freezes as Alexander and Rufus continue with their story.)

Rufus: I am so frightened! Should we even go to where Father is? Maybe the soldiers will grab us, also. They don't crucify children, do they?

Alexander: Be quiet and just blend in with the people going to see this man, and the two others. What a way to die — such a horrible death. They actually die of suffocation.

Rufus: Don't tell me these things! The things you tell me make me even more nervous.

(Alexander and Rufus freeze as Mother speaks.)

Mother: I felt so sorry for my boys each time I heard them discuss this. I was more sorry for them at the time than for my husband, Simon. And yet, Simon must have been very frightened for himself, carrying that crosspiece. I'm sure he was panicked by having the two boys there, for they were just young men at the time, alone in Jerusalem and wishing he could be with them. Yet, this man was going to die and he was dying in place of that robber and thief, Barabbas. This man looked like he was carrying the weight of the world instead of just a cross. Simon said that when this man looked at him, all he felt was the warmth of love. *(hesitates slightly)* Well, let's go back to listening to my sons' story.

(Mother freezes as Alexander and Rufus continue with their story.)

Rufus: We've been here a while, Alexander, and I still don't see Father. Maybe they are going to crucify him.

Alexander: Don't be ridiculous, Rufus. Father probably has to stay there to help whether he wants to or not. He'll be back with us. But just stay — what was the man saying? I thought I heard him say that he's thirsty. That must be it because they're putting a sponge on a reed.

Rufus: But, he's refusing it! I thought he had said other things, too. Didn't he speak to that woman at the foot of the cross? He's saying something else now even though he can hardly breathe.

Alexander: He said, "It is finished." What does that mean? I suppose I could ask someone.

Rufus: No! You said to blend in and not be noticed. Don't ask anyone. Father might tell us later. Oh look, Alexander, he looks like he's dead. And it's only three o'clock in the afternoon, but it's so dark.

Alexander: That soldier, a Centurion I think, just slid his sword into the man's side. Oh, there is blood and water both coming out. It's so dark, I can't see the cross. The ground is shaking. Now I'm afraid, too, Rufus!

Rufus: But Alexander, before it got so dark and these thunderstorms started, I thought I saw Father up there in back of the group of women. Can we go up that direction to find him?

Alexander: Let's just wait until the wind dies down and the earth quits shaking. Maybe it is Father, but maybe it's someone else.

(Alexander and Rufus freeze as Mother speaks.)

Mother: My sons later told me that the darkness at three o'clock in the afternoon was so frightening because it was like midnight and when the earth was moving and everything shaking because of it, they truly were horrified at the tumult. Then they said it finally started to clear and they were holding on to each other. Then they saw him.

(Mother freezes as Alexander and Rufus continue with their story.)

Rufus: It is Father! Let's go to him. Alexander? *(slowly and thoughtfully)* Alexander? Why are you waiting and looking at that dead man?

Alexander: *(hesitantly)* There is such an expression on his face. There is no agony, no fear. He looks like he is truly at peace. He must have been someone very special.

(Alexander and Rufus freeze as Mother speaks.)

Mother: *(turns away from watching Rufus and Alexander)* Later, Simon found his sons. Simon told them everything that Jesus had said and then he told them about the look and emotion that passed between him and this Jesus. Oh yes, Jesus. Years ago we gave ourselves to him. We knew right from that Sunday morning, or resurrection morning, who he was and that was the beginning of our worship of God through his only Son. *(thoughtfully)* The Son of God — hmmm. The very Son of God that we hold as Lord of our lives. My sons and I believe that Simon, my husband and their father, is with Jesus now. Oh, how I long to see them both — Simon and Jesus!

A few years after Jesus' resurrection, Alexander and Rufus became leaders of Christians in Rome, and then Rufus and Paul became close to each other. God bless us all as we continue to tell the story of Jesus Christ.

Mary Clopas

Easter Day
A Monologue

Mary Clopas

Character
Mary Clopas

Props
None required

Setting
None required

Costume
Use period costume

Mary Clopas: *(quietly and yet questioning)* He is risen — my Lord — my nephew, Jesus. There is new life for all of us. *(looks at congregation)* You probably don't know much about me. My name is Mary and I am married to Clopas. We, too, live in Nazareth, near our families. My sister is also named Mary, which was confusing many times. She is my younger sister and the mother of Jesus. I have watched Jesus grow from a toddler to his ministries at age thirty and to his death. But now I know he was *not* just the boy and the man I knew, but he *is* my Lord, the Messiah, and he's *alive*!

How can this be? He certainly did die on Friday. I know because we three were there at the foot of the cross; that is, his mother, Mary; Mary Magdalene; and myself. We saw him die and we stood there when the Centurion put that sword in Jesus' side. We had heard all his words before, especially to his mother and to his disciple, John, who was with us. She is under John's care now.

My sister followed Jesus in so much of his ministry. She was in the background and yet he knew she was there. I couldn't understand on Friday why he had to be killed, but Mary understood. I don't know how she handled being there, seeing Jesus in such pain and agony, hearing his breathing get more shallow, and knowing he was being tortured right there in front of her eyes. I was so worried about her, my sister. Mary is such a lovely person. She has a deep soul and is such a great listener. In recent months, she has finally told me of the angel, Gabriel, and her pregnancy with Jesus. At first I thought she had lost her mind. But I have come to believe that everything she has told me has been true.

I had given birth two months before Mary, so when she, Joseph, and Jesus came back from Egypt, our sons were very close and they loved to play together.

I can't believe it. He is risen!

There was that time not long ago when Jesus' friend, Lazarus, died, and days later, Jesus came to their house and he raised Lazarus from death and he told us to unbind him, to help Lazarus be free again.

Jesus didn't have to die, you know. He had the same free will as the rest of us. He could have decided to live and have a normal life, have a family, and continue as a carpenter. He was a good one, like his father, Joseph. God didn't *make* him die. Jesus chose to die in our place, each one of us. I can hardly keep my wits about me when I think of this, when I wonder at the love he has for each of us. When I think of that beating and those nail holes, I just cannot keep from crying, even on this wonderful resurrection morning.

He is risen! Say it with me: He is risen! He is risen! Again, so loudly that you really believe it: He is risen! Hallelujah!